INTO IMMATERIAL CULTURE

Vilém Flusser

Translated by Rodrigo Maltez Novaes

Metaflux

Adentrando a Cultura Imaterial

©1986 Vilém Flusser
© 2015 Miguel Gustavo Flusser

Edited and translated
from Portuguese by Rodrigo Maltez Novaes

1. Communication; 2. Philosophy; 3. Media Theory

First edition © 2015 Metaflux Publishing

Book design and layout by Chagrin

Text revision: Kenton Card

Published by Metaflux Publishing
www.metafluxpublishing.com

Distributed by Ingram Content Group
www.ingramcontent.com

ISBN 978-0-9933272-0-9

METAFLUX/VILÉM FLUSSER

The philosopher Vilém Flusser was born in Prague in 1920 but emigrated to Brazil, fleeing from Nazi persecution, at the outbreak of war in 1939, arriving in Rio de Janeiro at the end of 1940, with his wife and parents-in-law, after a short stay in London. The Flussers settled in São Paulo during the 1940s, where they lived for thirty two years. In the early years of the 1970s they moved back to Europe, settling first in Italy, and subsequently in Robion, France, where they lived until Vilém Flusser's untimely death in 1991 after a car crash, as he left Prague at the end of a symposium.

During the years he lived in Brazil, Flusser wrote for several Brazilian periodicals and taught at different academic institutions, among them, the University of São Paulo, the Brazilian Institute of Philosophy, and the Institute of Technology and Aeronautics. His first two books, *Lingua e Realidade* and *A História do Diabo*, were published in Brazil during the 1960s. In the late 1970s, and throughout the 1980s, Flusser travelled most of Europe lecturing and participating in conferences and symposia, during which time he published his most well-known titles. He came to prominence in the field of Media Philosophy after publishing his seminal book *Towards a Philosophy of Photography* in 1984, shortly followed by *Ins Universum der Technischen Bilder* in 1985, and *Die Schrift. Hat Schreiben Zukunft?* in 1987.

As a polyglot, Flusser wrote in four different languages, German, Portuguese, English, and French. The Metaflux/Vilém Flusser collection aims to present to an international readership, high quality translations of Flusser's Brazilian writings, including courses, monographs, essays, and letters, as well as works originally written in English by the author.

The Metaflux/Vilém Flusser collection is possible due to the generous support of Miguel Gustavo Flusser and the Flusser Brasil Network.

PREFACE

The four essays of this book were delivered as a series of lectures at the School of Communication and the Arts of the University of São Paulo in August 1986, one year after the publication of the first Brazilian edition of *Towards a Philosophy of Photography*, published as *A Filosofia da Caixa Preta*.

Through these four short essays, Flusser presents, *in nuce*, his communications theory. Their style is condensed, with a series of quick-fire sentences, which for a better understanding, are best read in conjunction with his major works of the same period. However, for a fist time reader of his work, these four lectures are a good introduction to some of Flusser's polemic and provocative concepts regarding human communication, its future, and its ethical, aesthetic, and epistemological implications; a vision that is paradoxically utopian and dystopian.

Preface	v
Alphabetic Culture	9
Crisis in Alphabetic Culture	17
Anti-Alphabetic Revolutions	25
Immaterial Culture	35

I

ALPHABETIC CULTURE

The alphanumeric code, which dominated Western communication until our fathers' generation, is currently threatened by partly illassimilated new codes. The problem that this cultural transition posits is not only a formal one; it also provokes emotions, mobilises prejudices, and may contribute towards a deepening of current sociopolitical tensions. Example: campaigns to teach literacy right at the instant when the alphabet is in decadence. The fact is that many are existentially engaged in the alphanumeric code, and are prepared to defend it, even if they admit the inadequacy of such a code to all the recently elaborated communication media. The four lectures that I propose to deliver seek to discuss the passionate climate that surrounds the subject. And in this first lecture, I shall seek to elucidate the fascination that emanates from the alphabet.

The alphanumeric code consists of letters, of numbers, and of some auxiliary symbols. The code's repertoire is fully exposed on the keys of a typewriter, however, on the typewriter, it is stored according to a different order to that which orders the alphanumeric store within the human memory. The numbers, of Hindu origin, and transmitted to the West by Arabs during the high Middle Ages, symbolise the concept of sets. Thus, the number "2" symbolises the concept of a set of "pairs" and the number "0" the concept of an empty set. The letters, of Semitic origin, probably from the Sinai in the fourth millennium, acquired their current form and approximately their current meaning, in the Syrian region during the first half of the second millennium BC. They signify the initial sound of the Semitic word that designates the object represented by the form of the letter. Therefore, the letter "A" symbolises the initial sound of the word *Aleph*, which means "bull," represented by the form of the letter. And the letter "B" symbolises the initial sound of the word *Beth*, which means "house," represented by the form of the two domes of the letter. Hence, numbers are "ideograms" (symbols of concepts), and letters are transcodified "pictograms" (originally pictorial symbols that have come to signify the sounds of spoken language). Whoever writes alphanumerically, mobilises two incongruent mental processes: symbolically manipulates concepts, and symbolically manipulates spoken language. This hybrid nature of the code is partially responsible for the fertility of thought articulated through it. There are texts in which numbers dominate (the ones of the so called exact sciences), and others dominated by letters (the ones of "literature *sensu stricto*"). I throw the problem of the hybridity of the code in your faces, without commenting on it, in order to suggest to you its radical nature. But I cannot leave this without saying that, once the alphanumeric code has been overcome, mental processes will undoubtedly develop, that were up until now repressed by letters: processes that are more familiar to mathematical thinking than to literal thinking, but different from mathematical thought because they will not be quantifying. Thought will no longer be incarcerated by letters; no longer chained to spoken language.

Now, let's consider this submission of thought to language because of letters. As we write alphanumerically, we are making visual an auditory message. We are visually notating thoughts, feelings, desires, and commands that are linguistically articulated. We are not codifying, but transcodifying. Spoken language intrudes between our texts and us. We then tend to confuse thinking with speaking, and mind with language. For example: we refer to the rules of thought as "logical" (that is: linguistic), we deify the Verb, and have constructed ideological, linguistic edifices, such as the Hegelian and Heideggerian ones. This ontological confusion between mind and language (of which even I fell victim, when I wrote *Lingua e Realidade*[1]), which characterises our culture since the prophets and the pre-Socratics, passing through Christianity and Islam, all the way until the frustrated attempts of Russell and Whitehead to reduce linguistic propositions down to mathematical ones, demands that we, the partially post-alphabetic ones, face the following question: what were the motives of the Syrian inventors of the alphabet in proposing such a dubious code? To what end did these forefathers of Western thought impose on us, this unnecessary diversion of thought through spoken language? Why can we not write directly, as we do with numbers, or as

---

1 Flusser, Vilém. *Lingua e Realidade* (Language and Reality), Herder, São Paulo, 1963.

the Chinese do, and as our children do with digital computers? Why letters?

I shall suggest two answers, the first being this: the code that was dominant before the invention of the alphabet was that of images, either two- or threedimensional, very elaborate, or conventionally simplified, as in the case of pictograms. Images – as mediations between humans, who produce them, and the concrete world in which they live – are subjected to the dialectic that is proper to every mediation: they tend to substitute that which is to be mediated. From maps of the world, they become screens that conceal the world, and humans, instead of using images in order to orient themselves in the world, start to act in the world in function of images. This inversion of the function of images: "humans act in the world in function of images" is called *idolatry*, and human action in the world in function of images is called *magic*.

The alphabetic code was invented as a weapon against idolatry and magic. Its purpose was to "explicate" images, to make them transparent for the concrete world, and thus to liberate humanity from the oppression they exert upon us. Therefore, to de-alienate humanity from their own product: from images. However, humanity already has a code (and it exists since time immemorial) apt to explicate images: spoken language. Spoken language speaks "about" [*sobre*[2]] images, it flows over them. Here is why the inventors of the alphabet resorted to spoken language in their iconoclastic engagement, an engagement

---

2 The Portuguese preposition *sobre* can mean "over," "above," and "about," depending on the context, much in the same way as the German *über*.

that is clear in the prophets: God is unimaginable, but He is perfectly audible, He speaks, and speaks... (*omer veomer JHVH*).

However, this first answer to the question "Why letters?" is not enough. Because as letters turn visible the sounds of spoken language, they modify the structure of language. They force spoken language to adapt to the unidimensionality of the line, and they abstract from spoken language a whole set of parameters, such as voice intonation and sound modulation. Effectively: the language written in letters is a new type of language, a type invented by the inventors of the alphabet. So that a second answer to the question "Why letters?" offers itself spontaneously: to discipline spoken language and to purify it. Before the invention of the alphabet speaking was indistinct, as if with a closed mouth, badly articulated, stammered, and the term "myth" has the same etymological root as the term "mute." To be sure: the Romantics and their successors seek wisdom in myths, and for seeking them, they fatally find them. But the inventors of the alphabet were not Romantics, and they invented letters in order to fight against mythical thought articulated by spoken language.

Both answers to the question "Why letters?" are complementary. Letters combat magic as they explicate images, and combat myths as they discipline spoken language. Therefore, when considered in their fulness, both answers delineate the *"forma mentis"* articulated by letters. This is the mentality of someone who is engaged in progressive explications, and in the demythologising of thought. The inventors of the alphabet created a code for this type of mentality, and it formulated itself ever more perfectly with the increased and continuous use of the alphabet. We are accustomed to refer to this type of mentality as "historical" consciousness. So that the last answer to the question "Why letters?" is this: to serve as the code for historical consciousness, and thus turn viable the history of the West (which is the only type of history *sensu stricto*). Certainly: the inventors of the alphabet were not aware of this, since in them, historical consciousness was still underdeveloped. We, the ones who are living the crisis of historical consciousness, are the ones that can affirm this.

Consider for an instant our letters: these articulations of historical consciousness, these springs of Western history. They are windows through which we glimpse the initial scene from which our culture emerged: the "A" shows us the sacred bull, the "B" the house of God, the "C" the camel's curvature laden with delicacies from the far East. But through the power of our consciousness, we transcodify letters from images into instruments in order to dominate language, and through it, our own mind. We impose dead letters upon the living body of language, so that like vampires, they may suck the life that pulsates in language and come to live a new type of life. From under the fingers of he who writes alphabetically, a new life seems to want to be born, and the amorous fight – the body wrestling between writer and spoken language, during which language is violated but also seduces its aggressor – is the climate in which poetry emerges. Our letters are the preferential weapons of the Western mind on the conquest for beauty, and that is why they are called *"beaux."*

But our engagement in letters is not only because of their poetic power. As we impose letters upon living language in order to suck from it new life, we will never find virgin language. The language that reaches us has already passed through the bed of several aggressors. Literature is a tide that comes to us from the depths of our history, a chiselled product of generations of manipulators of letters, and we are, in turn, challenged to impose upon it our own mark and to transmit it, thus enriched, on to subsequent generations. The language that flows through literature towards the future purifies itself and becomes continuously more elegant and refined, an instrument always more exact and precious for the articulation of the mind. Effectively: literary language (any literary language), is indescribably beautiful, wise, and good, since it stores so much search for the true, the good, and the beautiful. Every literary language of the West is a heritage that has been entrusted to us so that we may keep, preserve, and enrich it. We are engaged in letters because they are the strong safe and keys to this treasure.

The considerations that I have just proposed to you seek to transmit to you the fascination that emanates from the alphabet. And it is not necessary for us to be poets, not even to be modest writers (as in my case), in order to experience this fascination: it is enough to have been pupils of a primary school before the introduction of word processors. What the children learnt in the not so distant past, when spelling preceded the handling of digital keyboards, was to speak correctly. Children no longer learnt to speak their native language, but literary language: Oxford English, the French of the Encyclopædists, Luther's German, Dante's Italian, and the Portuguese of sonnets. As they learnt to spell, the children learnt how to assume responsibility for the history that nurtured them. An ontological abyss separated these children from the illiterate ones: they were initiated in the secrets of historical consciousness whilst the illiterate lived in the prehistoric regions of magic and myth. Letters are fascinating because they are symbols for the initiation into the history of the West.

Our Syrian elders, those proto-Jews from the second millennium BC, imposed upon our minds an uncomfortable straitjacket when they invented the alphabet – a rather irrational code – which obliges us to make a long journey through language on our way from thought towards the page. It is an inconvenient code, as it demands the knowledge of several languages from anyone who wishes to communicate with the whole of Western society. Inconvenient, above all, because it is illadapted for the artificial intelligences that are soon to be installed. For all these reasons, the alphabet is on its way to being abandoned as the dominant code of our culture. Within the current information revolution (which is an anti-Semitic revolution in the deepest meaning of this term, as it substitutes texts with images), the Syrian code is being substituted by more performatic codes. And this revolution is the consequence of a crisis in alphabetic culture, which has been brewing for a long time. The next lecture will deal with this crisis. However, I cannot end today without confessing the melancholia that takes hold of me when I contemplate the case of the alphabet.

II

CRISIS IN ALPHABETIC CULTURE

One of the possible ways through which we may approach Western history is to consider it as a dialectic between images and texts. Here is how this history would be told in such a case: it starts during the first half of the second millennium BC with the invention of the alphabet. The purpose of Alphabetic texts was to explicate images, in order to emancipate humanity from the oppression of idolatry and magic. Typical examples of these texts are the books of Moses and the ones of the Prophets – in fact, every alphabetic text acts structurally in function of the destruction of images – however, images resist the attack aimed at them by texts. As texts progressively explicate images, these in turn progressively illustrate texts. A typical example of such a quarrel is Classical Greece of the fifth century BC when images began to signify poetic and dramatic texts, and when Platonic philosophy began to explicitly attack images. During the course of this dialectic, Christianity emerged as an attempt of synthesis between text and image: the Holy texts explicate idolatrous magic, and are in turn, illustrated by images.

Typical examples of such an attempt of synthesis are illuminated manuscripts, but also Romanesque column capitals and Gothic stained glass windows, which illustrate particular passages from texts. With the invention of typography the image/text dialectic was disturbed. Texts, therefore impelled by their linear dynamic, started to progress without references to images, and tended towards becoming unimaginable. A typical example is any text of modern science. As for images, these started to be expelled from daily life, and to be enclosed in glorified ghettos of the type: museums. Thus, alphabetic culture *sensu stricto* was initiated, together with its correlate, *art*, in the modern sense of the term. This divorce between text and image (between conceptual and imagistic thought), resulted in a crisis of culture: unimaginable concepts tend to be empty, and nonconceptual imagination tends to be hallucinatory. In order to overcome this crisis of Western culture, a new type of image emerged, of which the first variety is photography. With this new type of images, alphabetic culture initiated its slow decadence: the dialectic that propels Western culture will extinguish itself. Note that under this focus, Western culture is supported by three points: the invention of the alphabet, the invention of typography, and the invention of photography. I shall seek now to deepen this model a little.

From the sociopolitical point of view, the image/text dialectic manifests itself as a struggle between the literates and the illiterates, with the literates making up the dominant class. The literates (scribes, priests, monks, scientists, technocrats), seek to manipulate the illiterates (serfs, pagans, villains, profanes, laymen) in function of texts, but the illiterates react in function of images. During this class struggle, the dominant texts penetrate the dominated images in order to be transcodified into images. Example: the Cult of Mary. And dominated images are absorbed by dominant texts in order to be transcodified into texts. Example: pagan feasts transcodified into Church feasts. The literates live with historical consciousness and act historically: they are the bearers of Western history. The illiterates live with magical consciousness and suffer the historic acts: they are the base that supports Western history. With the invention of typography, the literate class is amplified in two stages. First it includes the bourgeoisie, and after, with the introduction of compulsory schooling, the proletariat. This quantitative amplification of historical consciousness is followed by a qualitative impoverishment. The cheapening of texts results in a shallow historical consciousness, and the subsequent inflation of texts, results in the devaluation of historical consciousness into ideology. Finally, with the invention of photography, there emerges a new dominant class, with a new consciousness: that of image programmers.

From the epistemological point of view, the image/text dialectic manifests itself as a struggle between concept and idea. Text may be considered as an alignment of clear and distinct elements (either numbers or letters). These elements were pulled out, from confusing and indistinct contexts, in order to be aligned: in the case of numbers the context was the image, and in the one of letters it was spoken language. The Latin word *"legere,"* and the German *"lesen,"* mean to pullout from a confusing context in order to distinctly align. Effectively, texts mean the conception of a confusing context. Texts conceive images (ideas), as they tell the content of images: they are accounts and tales.[1] They are "calculations": they align stones, like the Abacus. The purpose of Western history, as alphabetic culture, is to conceive ideas, to count, to calculate, in sum: to transcodify the mind as a whole into alignments of clear and distinct elements. This purpose is progressively realised: image after image, idea after idea, are transcodified into text; they are "described." After the invention of typography, the tide of texts accelerates and develops calculating methods, elaborated *ad hoc*: modern science. At the end of the 18th century, a culminating moment for alphabetic culture, absolute knowledge, in the sense of a total calculability of the world and the mind, seemed to be within reach. Also at this culminating point, texts began to invert against themselves, in order to calculate their own structure (the critique of science as a critique of discursive reason). This inversion of the intention of texts (of no longer being a critique of ideas, but a critique of the critique of ideas), results in the computation of calculated elements. Instead of destroying images (explicating them), texts now began to build images (to compute them). The first image thus computed from clear and distinct concepts is photography. Which generates the emergence of a new type of post-textual knowledge: models.

From the cultural point of view (in the broadest sense of the term), the image/text dialectic manifests itself as a struggle

---

1 In Portuguese Flusser creates a play with the words *contas* and *contos*. *Contas* can be translated as both "beads" and "accounts" and *contos* as "tales" or "loose-change, small coins."

between discursive reason and irrationality. Texts are articulations of rationality, in the sense that "reason" means the piecing of the mind into clear and distinct rations. Images, in turn, are articulations of the imagination, in the sense that "to imagine" means to incorporate something into the mind's vision. During the course of the larger part of Western history, this mutual negation between discursive reason and imagination had a highly positive result: images became ever more rational, and texts ever more imaginative. There is nothing more rational than the images of the Enlightenment; nothing more imaginative than the texts of modern science. During the age of lights, such culminating point in our history, a point when reason was irrationally deified, the triumph of alphabetic culture seemed to be within reach: individuals, and society, apt to live reasonably in full delight of their imaginative capabilities. However, a rational attitude involves a critical attitude, not only in relation to imagination and the other mental faculties, but also in relation to rationality itself. The further discursive reason develops, the more it becomes critical of itself. Until it selfdestructs. This suicide of reason, whose ultimate victims are the ones of my generation, results in the emergence of a new post-rational and antirational irrationalism, which is supported by discursive reason. Thus, a new imagination emerges, supported by the concepts of reason in order to negate them. Photography is the first product this new type of irrationalism.

From the existential point of view, the image/text dialectic manifests itself as the struggle between doubt and trust. Text may be considered as the result of a methodical doubt in relation to the imagined: it decomposes the imagined into pixels and aligns such pixels methodically. Before the invention of typography, texts methodically doubted pretextual images: the Bible, for example, is a text that doubts the images of paganism. If Socrates was accused of lack of piety, he was accused because he opposed texts to images, thus, the Romans considered Judæo-Christianity as an illomened form of impiety. After the invention of the printing press, scientific texts started to doubt the prescientific ones, because they considered them to be infiltrated by images. G. Bruno corresponds to Socrates in this stage of our history, thus, the Judæo-Christians considered the Enlightenment as an illomened form of impiety. The Enlightenment, and somewhat anachronistically, the Russian Revolution, believed in the definitive victory of doubt over faith, of texts over images. However, despite Descartes, doubt is perfectly capable of doubting itself, and from the 19th century onwards, selfcritical texts started to enlighten Enlightenment itself. The result is a curious type of second degree trust, a curious type of faith in a distrust of doubt, which articulates itself through second degree images, and which we may observe on television screens. This second degree trust, such bad faith, existentially illustrates the victory of second degree images over texts.

Now I return to the model of Western culture that I proposed to you at the beginning of this lecture: the dialectic between text and image, having as focal points the invention of the alphabet, of typography, and of photography. According to this model, Western culture develops its dynamics within the phase between the alphabet and typography, between the first half of the second millennium BC and the 15th century. In its second phase, generally referred to as "The Modern Age," our culture would have reached, at least apparently, its maturity. Texts triumphed over images, society as a whole became literate, the world and humanity became calculable, individual and social life became reasonable, and methodical doubt destroyed all beliefs. The exact sciences started to dominate the cultural scene, and its consequence, *technics*, with its industrial revolution, allowed our culture to dominate the whole globe. For an observer from the age of lights, from the age of the American and French revolutions, alphabetic mentality seems to have triumphed, and the establishment of the Humanist paradise seems to be only a question of time. However, to us, postmodern observers, the Modern Age is already the bearer of the germ of our culture's decadence. The crisis of alphabetic culture already announces itself to us in the invention of typography, because as it eliminates images from daily life, typography liberates texts to invest against themselves and to selfdestruct. And the crisis of alphabetic culture shatters the surface with the invention of photography, in order to currently flood the scene in the form of technical images and the emergence of a new computing and programming mentality.

In the next lecture I shall deal with the emergence of this new post-alphabetic mentality, and in the fourth and last lecture I shall seek to project a vision of the utopian situation that is opening up for this new mentality. However, I cannot end these reflections without considering the impact that the decadence of alphabetic culture, of Western culture, is having on us. Certainly: our culture does not deserve to be wept for. It has committed crimes unequalled in the history of humanity, of which the enslavement of Africans and Auschwitz are only but a few examples. We must bury Cæsar, and not praise him. Having said this, we must know what we are burying, which are, in fact, the so-called values of the West; the values of Judæo-Christianity, Humanism, and the Enlightenment. However, even though the realisations of the West are, in their majority, regrettable, and even if they threaten the survival of humanity as a whole (such as the thermonuclear armament and the pollution of the world), their inherent values are still, nonetheless, admirable. Therefore, our challenge seems to be this: how can we pass from alphabetic culture to the new one, without sacrificing these inherent values as a whole?

What I have proposed to you in this lecture was a model of Western culture. On their own, models have no validity, and must be erased after being used. By the way, to say this is already a manifestation of this new mentality, which proposes and uses models without trusting them. Therefore, you must erase my model, just as all preceding models, irrespective of how sacred they may be, such as the Judæo-Christian, or Marxist ones. But models have validity, as long as they provoke new models. It is you, therefore, who will, or will not, confer value to the model I have proposed.

III

ANTI-ALPHABETIC REVOLUTIONS

In today's lecture, I shall work mainly with three concepts, and I shall temporarily give them the following names: first degree imagination, discursive reason, and second degree imagination, supported by discursive reason. In order to allow you to visualise my aim, I shall give you the following examples of phenomena that result from these three concepts: cave paintings at Lascaux, scientific texts, and images synthesised by computers. And I propose the following model: Western alphabetic culture emerged from a culture of first degree imagination, but currently, a new culture of second degree imagination is emerging from Western culture (and possibly also from the far East). What matters in this model is above all the distinction between these two types of imagination as cause; between the one that is responsible for the images of the type "Lascaux," and the one that is responsible for images of the type that are computed. If we cannot make this distinction, we will not grasp the revolution that is shaking us up.

I suggest that first degree imagination characterises the human species: *Homo sapiens sapiens* is an image-maker. Let us try to intuit how images are made. Humans, just like any other living being, are immersed within a circumstance that advances against them, and against which humanity advances. So we may say that humans, just like any other living being, are part of a given concrete world that is fourdimensional: space in movement. The human species previous to ours, managed to freeze part of the circumstance in movement when they produced instruments. The flint knife is frozen circumstance: still (understood, *verstanden*). The temporal dimension was abstracted from the knife. The species previous to ours, were human for having abstracted time from space, for having fixed instruments. The threedimensional, still circumstance, is palpable for the hands and visible for the eyes. But it is difficult for the eyes to orient themselves in it: this circumstance does not allow for an encompassing view. In order to reach such a view it is necessary for humans to take a step back from the circumstance, to distance themselves from it, to "alienate" themselves from it. Homo sapiens sapiens took that step. He retreated from the circumstance into his subjectivity and thus opened that abyss that separates us from the world. He managed to achieve this distanced view of the world, which the Germans call *"Weltanschauung."*

Let us consider the *Weltanschauung*: the world is no longer palpable, the hands no longer reach it. This is a world that is only apparent for the eyes; it is "phenomenal"; it deceives. This world is an imagined world that has lost its concretion, but has gained amplitude. Effectively: it is superficial and plane, the dimension of depth has been abstracted from it. The bidimensional world of the imagination allows itself to be used as a map for interventions in the threedimensional, concrete world. *Weltanschauung* orients praxis. However, in order to serve as a guideline for orientation, the *Weltanschauung* needs to be adapted. First degree imagination is swift and subjective. In order to serve as a map it needs to be fixed and intersubjectified. It may be fixed as it is projected upon the concrete world (for example, onto cave walls). The concrete world serves as a medium for subjective imagination. And in order to be intersubjectified, imagination may be codified. The code – intersubjective consensus – makes subjective imagination accessible to other subjects. Images are codified *Weltanschauungen* projected upon the concrete world. And first degree imagination is the ability to abstract one dimension from the concrete world, reproject such abstraction upon the world, and codify it.

Images serve as maps for action in the concrete world, however, given the internal dialectics of any mediation, they start to conceal the world. First degree imagination tends to be hallucinatory, and the actions informed by it tend to be ritual and inoperable. Western culture elaborated a code that is able to rupture the veil of imagination: the alphabetic and numeric codes, and their use, allowed for the development of discursive reason, which is the ability to analyse, to critique, to enumerate, to align, and to calculate. In sum: to count the content of images, of "ideas." The process of discursive reason consists of the following phases: images are decomposed into pixels and ideas into concepts. Concepts are ordered according to specific rules in order to form the lines of the discourse. And these lines of ordered concepts are integrated into sequences in order to form arguments. Within discursive reason, this is the recoding of first degree imagination, the recoding from plane to line. As much as the discourse may ramify and fan-out, its unidimensional structure will always be preserved. Discursive reason is more abstract than first degree imagination: it has one dimension missing.

The function of discursive reason is to explicate, to make explicit what is implicit in images. If all images were made explicit, if all ideas were analysed and critiqued, discursive reason would become inoperative. To aim towards an end is an integral part of the unidimensional nature of reason. Therefore, reason is structurally utopian: it demands perfection and the fullness of time. However, it is not this entelechial dynamism of reason that makes it "historical," in the strict sense of the term. The rules that order the concepts are univocal; they form unrepeatable chains, of which the chain of cause and effect is just one example. The famous reversibility of mathematical propositions is illusory, as Kant proved in analysing synthetic *a priori* propositions. Discursive reason is historical because its rules impose upon the mind a model of irreversible linear time, which flows, coming from the past, towards the future, dragging space with it. This dramatic nature of discursive reason (every instant is unique, and every opportunity lost is lost for ever), is the climate of our culture. The biggest triumph of discursive reason is exact science, and the acts that result from it: applied technics. Science is dramatic, as it tends to explicate all of the ideas in relation to the world and to humans within the world, and technics is the method for the realisation of the utopia: perfection and the fullness of time. The world, humans, and society, scientifically explicated and technically conducted, would be a reasonable paradise.

As it is codified alphanumerically, discursive reason projects its linear structure, and the rules that order its concepts through explicated images, upon the world and upon the mind. For a long time it was believed that this structure and these rules were not projected, but discovered by reason, and that the world and the mind somehow mysteriously reflect discursive reason. This adequation of reason to its object was believed to work, above all because of technics, a praxis informed by reason. However, currently, there is evidence being gathered, which suggests that reason is projected onto its object by the subject, just as much as images are. This evidence is gathering because reason has advanced with its analyses, critiques, and explications, into layers of the world and the mind, in which the structure and rules of reason refuse to apply. Thus, reason advanced up to the limits of its competence, precisely for being so efficient. Within these limits, trust in the explicatory capacity of reason becomes unreasonable, and the alphanumeric code stops being considered adequate to the structure of the object.

To put it very schematically, the inadequacy of such code to the object, or of discursive reason to the world and the mind, owes to the quantic character of the phenomena within deeper layers. Within these layers, punctual elements behave in leaps and not according to the rules of the discourse. Categories such as chance and symmetry, and not categories such as causality and sequence, are adequate to these layers. Examples: the behaviour of particles that constitute the nucleus of an atom is falsified, when described linearly, and the behaviour of bits of information that constitute the mind is falsified, when explained discursively. The progressive knowledge of cerebral functions, of the quantic leaps of particles above the intervals between the nervous synapses, insistently suggest that discursive reason, as well as first degree imagination (and all the other cerebral functions), are computations with punctual elements, a kind of mosaic made up of little pebbles. Imagination, codified into images, would be the computation of punctual elements in order to form planes, and discursive reason, alphanumerically codified, would be the computation of punctual elements in order to form lines.

This view of the world and mind as vacuities in which zerodimensional particles leap at random, demands that a new mental capacity and new codes be elaborated. I propose that we may call this new emerging capacity "second degree imagination," and that the new codes, through which this new imagination articulates itself, have already been elaborated: they are the digital codes, above all the binary ones, which we learn as we manipulate computers.

Here is how second degree imagination works: clear and distinct elements, of which rational thought is composed, are being pulled from their linear structure in order to be inserted into other structures. They form thus mosaics, generally of two dimensions (as in computer screens), but may equally acquire additional dimensions (as in the case of moving holograms). Strictly speaking, these are zerodimensional structures, since they are composed of punctual elements and intervals. This zerodimensionality justifies the term "immaterial," which has been applied to the culture that produces such manifestations of this new imagination. What matters, however, for a comprehension of this new consciousness behind these images, is not so much their mosaic structure, or their zerodimensionality, and not even the digital codes through which this new consciousness articulates itself. What matters, is the inversion of the vectors of significance, which the anti-alphabetic revolution operates.

First degree imagination produces images that represent the concrete world. To decipher such images is to discover in them what they represent. This is valid for both the so-called "figurative" images (the concrete world represented in them is the objective world), and for the so-called "abstract" images (the concrete world represented in them is the subjective world). Discursive reason produces texts that explicate the concrete world. To decipher such texts is to discover in them the problem that they explicate. In both cases, they are the signifier (first degree images and texts), and the world is the signified. However, this semantic analysis no longer applies to second degree images. They are projections onto the causal and absurd vacuity once called "world and mind," and their aim is to confer meanings (*Sinngebung*) to the absurd. They do not represent: they model. To decipher them is to discover in them the meaning intended. This deciphering does not seek the tip of the arrow of meaning (as in first degree images), but the bow that propels the arrow: the intention behind the images. The new imagination is intentional: it proposes, it does not represent. In synthetic images of mathematical equations, the character of this new mentality becomes obvious: they are propositions to reveal the meanings of the concepts of which the equations are composed. We, the ones that witness this revolution, still have not learned to decipher these new images adequately. Our second degree imagination is still underdeveloped, which explains the relative poverty of such images. Undoubtedly, however: a new horizon for creativity is opening up.

In the last lecture, I shall speak of this new horizon. I must, however, rectify the model that underlines the present lecture. The model was this: humans, just like any other living being, exist within a situation with four dimensions, in a situation where objects present themselves. The human species previous to ours, fixed some objects, produced instruments, and lived within a threedimensional circumstance, within objective culture. Our species introduced an imaginary zone between humans and the threedimensional circumstance, a bidimensional zone of first degree imagination. Western culture introduced a conceptual zone between humans and the imagined world, a unidimensional zone of alphanumerically codified explications. Currently, a new zone is emerging, a zerodimensional one, of computed and digitally codified images. The rectification to be made is this: the model is not a pyramid of univocal abstractions, a ladder that we climb step-by-step. On the contrary: as we live and think, we are constantly going up and down through the steps of abstraction, we remain on the lower steps for most of our lives, and we manage to fix ourselves onto the more abstract steps only for fleeting moments. Second degree imagination is a level of abstraction that is difficult to sustain, and we are being called upon in order to learn to live in it. That is the challenge, which the present hurls at us.

IV

IMMATERIAL CULTURE

The theme of this last of four lectures will be the brain, and I must therefore warn you that about neurophysiology, I understand almost next to nothing. This is my excuse: I shall speak about the brain in the same way that mechanist philosophers spoke of machines, and that Baroque thinkers spoke of clocks. And in these somewhat metaphorical uses, the ignorance of details helps: it allows thought to fly high. So please keep my ignorance in mind as you criticise me after the lecture.

I said that today's theme is the brain: I should have said that utopia will be the theme, because currently, these two subjects are entwined. My argument, during the last lectures, was that a new layer of consciousness – with new codes, and therefore, with new categories of thought, evaluation, and action – is emerging. I shall argue today that this utopian vision of the imminent future is connected to a type of image of the brain, and of the nervous system, in several different ways. Some examples: the post-industrial revolution is characterised by the installation of apparata that simulate cerebral functions and/or the functions of perceptive organs, that is, of cerebral organs. The digital code, which articulates this new imagination, simulates through its structure, the quantic leaps of particles inbetween the synapses. The brain, with its extremely complex structure and its intricately entwined functions, is the model *par excellence* of a black-box, and serves as the starting point for the cybernetic analyses of complex systems. The slow, but inexorable, diversion of our interest – which progressively abandons problems of the modification of the objective world (of work), towards problems of information (of data processing) – is in essence a diversion from the muscular and digestive systems, towards the nervous system. And the concept of cerebral orgasm, also diverts our interest from the reproductive system. The social fabric, once viewed as a battlefield of interests, is progressively visualised as a neural net. And above all: concrete reality is no longer experienced as something solid that bars our path with its inert perfidy, but as an absurd vacuity, ruled by blind chance and comparable with the computational intervals between the cerebral nerves. These multipliable examples may be summarised *ad nauseam*: the utopian vision is connected to the view of the brain, because both are visions where the material and the mental are confused with each other. The next São Paulo Biennial has utopia as a central concept: I suggest that they should use a synthetic image of the brain as a logo.

I shall start my utopian reflections from the sociopolitical field, because politics deals with power, that is: with decisions and freedom, and every utopia, including the negative ones, deal with freedom. Under a Darwinian focus (be it coloured by liberalism on the "right," or by socialism on the "left"), there is a struggle for power, and those who gain power decide for others. I argued during the last lectures that such a linear, processual, discursive, and historical focus is no longer sustainable. Currently, decisions can be decomposed into bits-of-decision and recomputed as mosaic-decisions, a strategy through which artificial intelligences make decisions. There is no individual, group, class, or grey-eminence that retains the power of decision, because such power is not something that could be retained. Example: if the north American President and/or the General Secretary of the Communist Party were to decide to press the red button and reduce culture to radioactive ash, they would not be exercising their power of decision, but executing an individual act provoked by other individual acts, for example, by a button being pressed on a TV screen that shows missiles flying towards the USA and/or the USSR. That is why the function of American President and/or General Secretary of the Communist Party may be perfectly robotised. The President and the Secretary are not powerful, but functionaries of an automatic apparatus that may be ever more automated. Classic, linear, and historical political thought, must give way to cybernetic thought, a term in whose root the verb "*kybernein*" is found, from which the term "to govern" also derives. Political Darwinism must give way to a neurophysiological view of society.

Within the brain, there are no zones, no special functions, no central point that governs the rest, and that makes definitive decisions. The decisions taken by the brain (that is: by us as individuals) are the result of the computation of decisivebits that occur all over the brain. Decisions are taken by something that may be called "consensus." The same occurs in society, this superbrain composed of brains, with the only difference being that society is a very inefficient brain. And because of such inefficiency, we nurture the illusion that there are those who make decisions and those who are manipulated. The utopian vision projects an image of society as a better structured superbrain. A society without government, with the power of decision being diluted throughout the social net, therefore a free society, however, with a new, interrelational, ludic meaning of the term "freedom." This utopian, cerebralising vision of society is already technically viable (which does not imply that it is effectively viable). The technical knowledge that allows for the establishment of such a utopian society is called "telematics," and now I shall divert the argument to this field.

I shall not deal with the theoretical aspects of telematics, such as decision theory or game theory. I shall not do it simply for the lack of time. I shall only sketch out the results of applied telematics. It is a net of reversible cables, and at each crossing point, or knot, can be found artificial and human intelligences. The cables carry information that are processed and reprocessed at the crossings. The input of the net is data that comes from the external and internal worlds (from "matter" and "mind"). The output of the net are decisions transmitted to machines, decisions whose purpose is to give meaning to the external and internal worlds, that is: to the lives of the participants of the telematised game. (This was, shall we say, an "ontological" statement, before we consider the social superbrain a little closer.) The classic question, "Is society a system at the service of the individual, or is the individual a particle of society that functions socially?" is overcome. Neither society, nor the individual, are concretely given. What is concrete, is the intersubjective relation (the "cable"), of which society and the individual are nothing but horizons. It no longer makes sense to try to distinguish between artificial and human intelligence, and it will continuously make less sense, because concrete reality is not in them, but in the informational relations that link them. This "ontological" statement is easier to say than to experience. That is because we still do not live in such utopia.

Note that the telematic net not only puts an end to the notions of individual and society; it also ends with the notions of public and private. It ends, therefore, with the notion of unhappy consciousness, that which hangs between the public in order to lose itself, and the private in order to lose the world. The information travels the intervals between individuals through cables, and in doing so, they synchronise space and annihilate time: "utopia" means precisely lack of space, therefore, time stood still. In such a situation there is neither public nor private space: all the participants of telematics are contemporaries and neighbours. Note even that the telematic net establishes a present that stands still, a kind of *"nunc stans."* The information that travels the reversible cables go from memory to memory, and all of their variants are stored and retrievable. As a challenge to the second law of thermodynamics, no information is lost, unless it is deliberately deleted. This implies that the past is always present and that the future is the past represented.

This is what post-history is. This challenge to the second law (which is the reason for every mental process) is not, however, a miracle that ends with the tendency of things to progress towards entropy. This is possible because the telematics society is "immaterial" culture, that is, a culture that no longer stores elaborated information in objects. Perishable and forgettable works no longer exist in such a culture; there is only the flux of bits of information that are stored electromagnetically and audiovisually retrievable. Certainly: the cables that carry the information, which are currently made of inorganic material (but which eventually will be made of nerve-like material), are perishable. Therefore the knots of the net are also perishable, whether they are human brains or computers. We are not yet immortal in such utopia. But this is of little importance, since the information elaborated by the knots (by us or the artificial intelligences), are imperishable. Which, in the end, seems very close to the notion of immortality of both the Jews, *zecher*, and the Greeks, *mnemosine*. In sum: the key aspect of the telematics utopia is imperishable processing memories.

Now I shall pick-up the argument from the preceding lecture, in which I developed the concept of second degree imagination. The telematic game that I have just sketched, whose aim would be to give meaning to the participants' lives, and turn them immortal within imperishable memories, will result in images that are synthesised dialogically by those who participate in such society. These synthetic images, these computations of clear and distinct concepts, in order to become models for the projection of meaning, will be the dominant cultural products of future society. Second degree imagination is no longer the faculty of an individual mind, as first degree imagination is, however, it will be an intersubjective faculty: the new images will be the product of the dialogic collaboration between artificial and human intelligences. And the digital codes – through which such images will be articulated, these codes that operate with punctual elements, as does the brain – will be the dominant code of future culture, thus taking the place of the alphanumeric code of the present Western culture. Second degree imagination will, therefore, be a level of consciousness that breaks through the shell of individuality in order to penetrate the territory of intersubjectivity, just as cerebral processes break through the cranial shell and are observable, as if inside out, in microchips. The once-called "mental" processes, like imagination and discursive reason, will become immaterial processes within that grey zone between mind and matter that the new technics turn accessible. And it is this grey zone, the destroyer of historical categories, which will be the territory of the new culture.

I have unveiled a utopian vision of telematic, immaterial culture, in which *Homo ludens* will dedicate his lifetime to creativity born out of a second degree imagination, rested upon clear and distinct reason, within a society driven cybernetically through intersubjective feedback; a society without governance or power, a society of freedom. All of the technical prerequisites for the establishment of such a culture are already here: nothing needs to be invented; it is only necessary to distribute the existing apparata and to allow society to make use of them. However, I do not believe for even one instant that such a culture will be realised. The reason for my disbelief are not so much the probable catastrophes that will curtail the realisation of such an inebriating project: the thermonuclear threat, the pollution of the Earth's environment, or the justified, although irrational, revolt of the Third World. My disbelief in this utopia is not even related to the reasons inherent in the project itself, for example, everyone's refusal to play in the creative game for the endowment of meaning to the absurdity of life. I do not believe in the realisation of the project because I am convinced that accidents always intervene in the realisation of no matter what project, and that such accidents are, by definition, unpredictable. By the way, the unpredictability of accidents is the very essence of freedom. Therefore, the question emerges: with what aim did I present this utopian project and these four lectures, if not as an introduction to such project?

I do not know if the answer to this question, which I propose with the highest honesty that I am capable of, will be considered satisfactory by you, but here it is: I believe that to engage oneself in projects that are known to be unrealisable but desirable, and to seek to convince others to also engage in such projects, turns such projects a little less unrealisable, and I do not know of any other type of engagement more worthy of its name. But I would like to close this course of lectures with the following consideration: I have spoken of intersubjectivity as a concrete reality, in which interlinked subjects are nothing more than abstract horizons. Respectively, such instersubjective relation is the only concrete reality to which we can hang on to within a situation where everything formerly held as real (the objective world and the world of the mind) dissipates into vacuity. However, this intersubjective relation already has an ancient name, although worn-out, and turned kitsch: *Love*.

This book was designed and composed
with Montserrat and Borgia Pro.

Metaflux ©2015

ISBN 978-0-9933272-0-9

www.ingramcontent.com/pod-product-compliance
Lightning Source LLC
Chambersburg PA
CBHW051959290426
44110CB00015B/2307